50 Premium Be Recipes

By: Kelly Johnson

Table of Contents

- Beef Wellington
- Prime Rib Roast
- Braised Short Ribs
- Filet Mignon with Red Wine Reduction
- Beef Bourguignon
- Korean Beef Bulgogi
- Beef Stroganoff
- Grilled Flank Steak with Chimichurri
- Beef Tenderloin with Gorgonzola Cream Sauce
- Osso Buco
- Beef Enchiladas
- Italian Beef Sandwiches
- Classic Beef Tacos
- Barbecue Brisket
- Beef and Mushroom Pie
- Beef and Vegetable Stir-Fry
- Thai Beef Salad
- Stuffed Bell Peppers with Ground Beef
- Beef Fajitas
- Beef and Guinness Stew
- Beef and Broccoli Stir-Fry
- Beef Kofta Kebabs
- Beef Chili with Beans
- Beef Ragu with Pappardelle
- Grilled Ribeye Steaks
- Beef Kebab with Yogurt Sauce
- Beef Pot Roast with Vegetables
- Smoked Beef Tenderloin
- Beef Tamales
- Beef Picadillo
- Beef and Barley Soup
- Szechuan Beef with Peppers
- Beef Casserole with Cheese Topping
- Beef Satay with Peanut Sauce
- Beef Tartar with Capers

- Beef and Mushroom Stroganoff
- Beef and Pepper Stir-Fry
- Thai Red Curry Beef
- Beef Empanadas
- Beef Shakshuka
- Beef Jalfrezi
- Beef Brisket Tacos
- Beef and Lentil Stew
- Beef and Bacon Burgers
- Beef and Sweet Potato Hash
- Moroccan Beef Tagine
- Beef and Spinach Stuffed Shells
- Beef and Avocado Salad
- Beef and Artichoke Pasta
- Beef Rendang

Beef Wellington

Ingredients:

- 2 lb beef tenderloin
- Salt and pepper, to taste
- 2 tablespoons olive oil
- 1 lb mushrooms, finely chopped
- 4 oz pâté (optional)
- 8 slices prosciutto
- 1 sheet puff pastry
- 1 egg, beaten (for egg wash)

Instructions:

1. **Prepare the Beef**: Season beef tenderloin with salt and pepper. Heat olive oil in a skillet and sear the beef on all sides. Remove from heat and let it cool.
2. **Prepare the Mushroom Duxelles**: In the same skillet, add chopped mushrooms and cook until moisture evaporates. Let it cool.
3. **Assemble**: Lay out prosciutto on a sheet of plastic wrap. Spread pâté (if using) over prosciutto, then add mushroom duxelles. Place the beef on top and roll tightly using the plastic wrap. Chill for 30 minutes.
4. **Wrap in Pastry**: Roll out puff pastry and wrap around the beef, sealing edges. Brush with egg wash.
5. **Bake**: Preheat oven to 400°F (200°C). Bake for 25-30 minutes or until golden brown. Let it rest before slicing.

Prime Rib Roast

Ingredients:

- 5 lb prime rib roast
- Salt and pepper, to taste
- 4 cloves garlic, minced
- 2 tablespoons rosemary, chopped
- 2 tablespoons olive oil

Instructions:

1. **Prepare the Roast**: Preheat oven to 450°F (230°C). Rub prime rib with olive oil, garlic, rosemary, salt, and pepper.
2. **Roast**: Place the roast in a roasting pan and roast for 20 minutes. Lower the temperature to 325°F (165°C) and roast for an additional 1.5 to 2 hours or until desired doneness.
3. **Rest and Serve**: Remove from oven, let rest for 20 minutes before slicing.

Braised Short Ribs

Ingredients:

- 3 lb beef short ribs
- Salt and pepper, to taste
- 2 tablespoons olive oil
- 1 onion, chopped
- 2 carrots, chopped
- 2 celery stalks, chopped
- 4 cloves garlic, minced
- 2 cups beef broth
- 1 cup red wine
- 2 tablespoons tomato paste

Instructions:

1. **Sear the Ribs**: Preheat oven to 325°F (165°C). Season short ribs with salt and pepper. In a large Dutch oven, heat olive oil and sear ribs on all sides.
2. **Add Vegetables**: Remove ribs and sauté onion, carrots, celery, and garlic until softened.
3. **Braise**: Add beef broth, red wine, and tomato paste. Return ribs to pot. Cover and braise in the oven for 2.5 to 3 hours until tender.

Filet Mignon with Red Wine Reduction

Ingredients:

- 4 filet mignon steaks
- Salt and pepper, to taste
- 2 tablespoons olive oil
- 1 cup red wine
- 1/2 cup beef broth
- 2 tablespoons butter

Instructions:

1. **Cook the Steaks**: Season filet mignon with salt and pepper. Heat olive oil in a skillet and sear steaks for 4-5 minutes per side for medium-rare. Remove and let rest.
2. **Make the Reduction**: In the same skillet, add red wine and beef broth, scraping the bottom to deglaze. Reduce by half, then stir in butter until melted.
3. **Serve**: Plate the filet mignon and drizzle with the red wine reduction.

Beef Bourguignon

Ingredients:

- 2 lb beef chuck, cut into cubes
- Salt and pepper, to taste
- 2 tablespoons olive oil
- 4 slices bacon, chopped
- 1 onion, chopped
- 2 carrots, sliced
- 4 cloves garlic, minced
- 2 cups red wine
- 2 cups beef broth
- 1 tablespoon tomato paste
- 2 bay leaves
- 1 teaspoon thyme

Instructions:

1. **Brown the Beef**: Preheat oven to 325°F (165°C). Season beef with salt and pepper. In a Dutch oven, heat olive oil and brown beef in batches. Remove and set aside.
2. **Cook Bacon and Vegetables**: In the same pot, cook bacon until crispy. Add onion, carrots, and garlic, sautéing until softened.
3. **Braise**: Return beef to pot and add red wine, beef broth, tomato paste, bay leaves, and thyme. Bring to a simmer, cover, and braise in the oven for 2-3 hours until tender.

Korean Beef Bulgogi

Ingredients:

- 1 lb beef sirloin, thinly sliced
- 1/4 cup soy sauce
- 2 tablespoons brown sugar
- 2 tablespoons sesame oil
- 4 cloves garlic, minced
- 1 tablespoon ginger, grated
- 1 green onion, chopped
- Sesame seeds for garnish

Instructions:

1. **Marinate the Beef**: In a bowl, combine soy sauce, brown sugar, sesame oil, garlic, ginger, and green onion. Add sliced beef and marinate for at least 30 minutes.
2. **Cook**: Heat a skillet over medium-high heat. Cook marinated beef for 5-7 minutes until browned.
3. **Serve**: Garnish with sesame seeds and serve with rice.

Beef Stroganoff

Ingredients:

- 1 lb beef sirloin, sliced
- Salt and pepper, to taste
- 2 tablespoons olive oil
- 1 onion, chopped
- 8 oz mushrooms, sliced
- 2 tablespoons flour
- 1 cup beef broth
- 1 cup sour cream
- Egg noodles for serving

Instructions:

1. **Cook the Beef**: Season beef with salt and pepper. In a skillet, heat olive oil and brown the beef. Remove and set aside.
2. **Sauté Vegetables**: In the same skillet, sauté onion and mushrooms until tender. Sprinkle flour and cook for 1 minute.
3. **Add Broth and Sour Cream**: Stir in beef broth and simmer. Add sour cream and return beef to skillet.
4. **Serve**: Serve over cooked egg noodles.

Grilled Flank Steak with Chimichurri

Ingredients:

- 1 lb flank steak
- Salt and pepper, to taste
- 1/4 cup olive oil
- 1/4 cup red wine vinegar
- 1 cup fresh parsley, chopped
- 3 cloves garlic, minced
- 1 teaspoon red pepper flakes

Instructions:

1. **Marinate the Steak**: Season flank steak with salt and pepper. In a bowl, mix olive oil, red wine vinegar, parsley, garlic, and red pepper flakes. Marinate steak for at least 1 hour.
2. **Grill**: Preheat grill to medium-high. Grill steak for 5-7 minutes on each side for medium-rare.
3. **Serve**: Let rest before slicing against the grain and serving with extra chimichurri.

Beef Tenderloin with Gorgonzola Cream Sauce

Ingredients:

- 2 beef tenderloin steaks
- Salt and pepper, to taste
- 2 tablespoons olive oil
- 1/2 cup heavy cream
- 1/4 cup Gorgonzola cheese, crumbled
- 1 tablespoon fresh parsley, chopped

Instructions:

1. **Cook the Steaks**: Season beef tenderloin with salt and pepper. Heat olive oil in a skillet over medium-high heat and sear steaks for 4-5 minutes per side for medium-rare. Remove and let rest.
2. **Make the Sauce**: In the same skillet, add heavy cream and Gorgonzola cheese. Stir until cheese melts and sauce thickens.
3. **Serve**: Slice the tenderloin and drizzle with Gorgonzola cream sauce. Garnish with parsley.

Osso Buco

Ingredients:

- 4 veal shanks (or beef shanks)
- Salt and pepper, to taste
- 1/4 cup flour
- 2 tablespoons olive oil
- 1 onion, chopped
- 2 carrots, chopped
- 2 celery stalks, chopped
- 4 cloves garlic, minced
- 1 cup white wine
- 2 cups beef broth
- 1 tablespoon tomato paste
- 1 bay leaf
- Zest of 1 lemon (for gremolata)
- 1/4 cup fresh parsley, chopped (for gremolata)

Instructions:

1. **Brown the Shanks**: Season veal shanks with salt and pepper and dredge in flour. In a large Dutch oven, heat olive oil and brown the shanks on all sides. Remove and set aside.
2. **Sauté Vegetables**: In the same pot, add onion, carrots, celery, and garlic, sautéing until softened.
3. **Braise**: Deglaze with white wine, scraping the bottom. Add beef broth, tomato paste, bay leaf, and return shanks to the pot. Cover and braise in the oven at 325°F (165°C) for about 2 hours until tender.
4. **Prepare Gremolata**: Mix lemon zest and parsley together.
5. **Serve**: Plate osso buco and sprinkle with gremolata.

Beef Enchiladas

Ingredients:

- 1 lb ground beef
- 1 onion, chopped
- 2 cloves garlic, minced
- 2 cups enchilada sauce
- 8 tortillas
- 2 cups shredded cheese (cheddar or Mexican blend)
- 1 teaspoon cumin
- Salt and pepper, to taste

Instructions:

1. **Cook the Beef**: In a skillet, cook ground beef with onion, garlic, cumin, salt, and pepper until browned.
2. **Assemble Enchiladas**: Preheat oven to 350°F (175°C). Spread a little enchilada sauce in a baking dish. Fill each tortilla with beef mixture, roll, and place seam side down in the dish.
3. **Add Sauce and Cheese**: Pour remaining enchilada sauce over the rolled tortillas and top with shredded cheese.
4. **Bake**: Bake for 20-25 minutes until cheese is melted and bubbly.

Italian Beef Sandwiches

Ingredients:

- 2 lb beef chuck roast
- Salt and pepper, to taste
- 1 cup beef broth
- 1 tablespoon Italian seasoning
- 4 rolls
- Giardiniera (pickled vegetables) for topping

Instructions:

1. **Cook the Beef**: Season chuck roast with salt and pepper. Place in a slow cooker with beef broth and Italian seasoning. Cook on low for 8 hours or until tender.
2. **Shred the Beef**: Remove the roast, shred the meat, and return it to the juices.
3. **Assemble Sandwiches**: Serve on rolls topped with giardiniera.

Classic Beef Tacos

Ingredients:

- 1 lb ground beef
- 1 packet taco seasoning
- 8 taco shells
- Toppings: shredded lettuce, diced tomatoes, shredded cheese, salsa

Instructions:

1. **Cook the Beef**: In a skillet, cook ground beef until browned. Drain excess fat. Add taco seasoning and water as directed on the packet. Simmer until thickened.
2. **Assemble Tacos**: Fill taco shells with seasoned beef and desired toppings.

Barbecue Brisket

Ingredients:

- 4 lb beef brisket
- Salt and pepper, to taste
- 2 cups barbecue sauce
- 1 tablespoon paprika
- 1 tablespoon garlic powder
- 1 tablespoon onion powder

Instructions:

1. **Prepare the Brisket**: Preheat oven to 300°F (150°C). Season brisket with salt, pepper, paprika, garlic powder, and onion powder.
2. **Roast**: Place brisket in a roasting pan, cover with foil, and roast for 4-5 hours or until tender.
3. **Serve**: Brush with barbecue sauce before serving.

Beef and Mushroom Pie

Ingredients:

- 1 lb ground beef
- 8 oz mushrooms, sliced
- 1 onion, chopped
- 2 tablespoons flour
- 1 cup beef broth
- 1 sheet puff pastry
- 1 egg (for egg wash)

Instructions:

1. **Cook Filling**: In a skillet, cook ground beef, mushrooms, and onion until browned. Stir in flour and beef broth, cooking until thickened.
2. **Assemble Pie**: Preheat oven to 400°F (200°C). Pour filling into a pie dish and cover with puff pastry. Cut slits for steam to escape. Brush with beaten egg.
3. **Bake**: Bake for 25-30 minutes or until golden brown.

Beef and Vegetable Stir-Fry

Ingredients:

- 1 lb beef sirloin, thinly sliced
- 2 cups mixed vegetables (bell peppers, broccoli, carrots)
- 3 tablespoons soy sauce
- 2 tablespoons sesame oil
- 2 cloves garlic, minced

Instructions:

1. **Cook the Beef**: In a hot skillet or wok, add sesame oil and cook the sliced beef until browned. Remove from pan.
2. **Sauté Vegetables**: In the same pan, add garlic and mixed vegetables, stir-frying until tender-crisp.
3. **Combine**: Return beef to the pan, add soy sauce, and stir until heated through. Serve over rice or noodles.

Thai Beef Salad

Ingredients:

- 1 lb beef flank steak
- Salt and pepper, to taste
- 4 cups mixed greens
- 1 cucumber, sliced
- 1 bell pepper, sliced
- 1/4 cup fresh cilantro, chopped
- 1/4 cup lime juice
- 2 tablespoons fish sauce
- 1 tablespoon sugar

Instructions:

1. **Cook the Steak**: Season flank steak with salt and pepper. Grill or pan-sear for 5-7 minutes per side for medium-rare. Let it rest, then slice thinly.
2. **Prepare Dressing**: In a bowl, whisk together lime juice, fish sauce, and sugar.
3. **Assemble Salad**: In a large bowl, combine greens, cucumber, bell pepper, cilantro, and sliced beef. Drizzle with dressing and toss gently before serving.

Stuffed Bell Peppers with Ground Beef

Ingredients:

- 4 large bell peppers (any color)
- 1 lb ground beef
- 1 cup cooked rice
- 1 cup diced tomatoes (canned or fresh)
- 1 onion, chopped
- 2 cloves garlic, minced
- 1 teaspoon Italian seasoning
- Salt and pepper, to taste
- 1 cup shredded cheese (cheddar or mozzarella)

Instructions:

1. **Preheat Oven**: Preheat the oven to 375°F (190°C).
2. **Prepare Peppers**: Cut the tops off the bell peppers and remove the seeds. Place them in a baking dish.
3. **Cook Filling**: In a skillet, cook the ground beef, onion, and garlic over medium heat until browned. Drain excess fat. Stir in cooked rice, diced tomatoes, Italian seasoning, salt, and pepper.
4. **Stuff Peppers**: Fill each bell pepper with the beef mixture. Top with shredded cheese.
5. **Bake**: Cover with foil and bake for 30 minutes. Remove foil and bake for an additional 10 minutes, until cheese is bubbly.

Beef Fajitas

Ingredients:

- 1 lb flank steak
- 1 tablespoon olive oil
- 1 bell pepper, sliced
- 1 onion, sliced
- 2 tablespoons fajita seasoning
- Tortillas (flour or corn)
- Optional toppings: salsa, guacamole, sour cream

Instructions:

1. **Marinate the Steak**: In a bowl, toss flank steak with olive oil and fajita seasoning. Let it marinate for at least 30 minutes.
2. **Cook Steak**: Heat a grill or skillet over medium-high heat. Cook the steak for 5-7 minutes per side for medium-rare. Let rest, then slice thinly.
3. **Sauté Vegetables**: In the same skillet, add bell pepper and onion. Sauté until softened.
4. **Serve**: Serve sliced steak and sautéed vegetables in tortillas with desired toppings.

Beef and Guinness Stew

Ingredients:

- 2 lbs beef chuck, cut into cubes
- Salt and pepper, to taste
- 2 tablespoons olive oil
- 1 onion, chopped
- 2 carrots, sliced
- 2 stalks celery, chopped
- 3 cloves garlic, minced
- 2 cups Guinness beer
- 4 cups beef broth
- 1 tablespoon Worcestershire sauce
- 2 bay leaves
- 2 teaspoons thyme

Instructions:

1. **Brown the Beef**: Season beef with salt and pepper. In a large pot, heat olive oil and brown beef cubes in batches. Remove and set aside.
2. **Sauté Vegetables**: In the same pot, add onion, carrots, celery, and garlic. Sauté until softened.
3. **Add Liquid**: Return beef to the pot. Add Guinness, beef broth, Worcestershire sauce, bay leaves, and thyme. Bring to a boil.
4. **Simmer**: Reduce heat and simmer for 1.5 to 2 hours, until beef is tender.

Beef and Broccoli Stir-Fry

Ingredients:

- 1 lb beef sirloin, thinly sliced
- 2 cups broccoli florets
- 2 tablespoons soy sauce
- 2 tablespoons oyster sauce
- 1 tablespoon cornstarch
- 2 tablespoons vegetable oil
- 2 cloves garlic, minced
- Cooked rice, for serving

Instructions:

1. **Marinate the Beef**: In a bowl, combine beef with soy sauce, oyster sauce, and cornstarch. Let marinate for 15 minutes.
2. **Cook Beef**: Heat vegetable oil in a skillet over high heat. Add beef and cook until browned. Remove and set aside.
3. **Stir-Fry Broccoli**: In the same skillet, add broccoli and garlic, stir-frying for 3-4 minutes.
4. **Combine**: Return beef to the skillet, stir to combine, and cook for an additional 2 minutes. Serve over rice.

Beef Kofta Kebabs

Ingredients:

- 1 lb ground beef
- 1 onion, grated
- 2 cloves garlic, minced
- 1 teaspoon ground cumin
- 1 teaspoon ground coriander
- 1/2 teaspoon cayenne pepper
- Salt and pepper, to taste
- Skewers (soaked if wooden)

Instructions:

1. **Prepare the Mixture**: In a bowl, combine ground beef, grated onion, garlic, spices, salt, and pepper. Mix well.
2. **Form Kebabs**: Divide the mixture into portions and shape onto skewers.
3. **Cook**: Preheat a grill or skillet over medium-high heat. Cook kebabs for about 10-12 minutes, turning occasionally, until cooked through.

Beef Chili with Beans

Ingredients:

- 1 lb ground beef
- 1 onion, chopped
- 2 cloves garlic, minced
- 1 can (15 oz) kidney beans, drained
- 1 can (15 oz) black beans, drained
- 1 can (28 oz) diced tomatoes
- 2 tablespoons chili powder
- 1 teaspoon cumin
- Salt and pepper, to taste

Instructions:

1. **Cook the Beef**: In a large pot, cook ground beef with onion and garlic until browned. Drain excess fat.
2. **Add Ingredients**: Stir in beans, diced tomatoes, chili powder, cumin, salt, and pepper.
3. **Simmer**: Bring to a boil, then reduce heat and simmer for 30 minutes.

Beef Ragu with Pappardelle

Ingredients:

- 1 lb beef chuck, cut into chunks
- 1 onion, chopped
- 2 carrots, chopped
- 2 cloves garlic, minced
- 1 cup red wine
- 2 cups beef broth
- 1 can (14 oz) crushed tomatoes
- Salt and pepper, to taste
- 1 lb pappardelle pasta
- Grated Parmesan, for serving

Instructions:

1. **Brown the Beef**: In a large pot, brown beef chunks over medium-high heat. Remove and set aside.
2. **Sauté Vegetables**: In the same pot, add onion, carrots, and garlic. Sauté until softened.
3. **Add Liquid**: Return beef to the pot. Pour in wine, broth, and crushed tomatoes. Season with salt and pepper.
4. **Simmer**: Cover and simmer for 2-3 hours until beef is tender.
5. **Cook Pasta**: Cook pappardelle according to package instructions. Serve ragu over pasta with grated Parmesan.

Grilled Ribeye Steaks

Ingredients:

- 2 ribeye steaks
- Salt and pepper, to taste
- 2 tablespoons olive oil
- Optional: garlic powder, fresh herbs for seasoning

Instructions:

1. **Prepare Steaks**: Season ribeye steaks with salt, pepper, and any additional seasonings. Brush with olive oil.
2. **Preheat Grill**: Preheat the grill to high heat.
3. **Grill Steaks**: Cook steaks for 4-6 minutes per side for medium-rare, adjusting time for desired doneness.
4. **Rest and Serve**: Let steaks rest for a few minutes before slicing.

Beef Kebab with Yogurt Sauce

Ingredients:

- 1 lb ground beef
- 1 onion, grated
- 2 cloves garlic, minced
- 1 teaspoon cumin
- 1 teaspoon paprika
- Salt and pepper, to taste
- Skewers (soaked if wooden)
- **For Yogurt Sauce**: 1 cup yogurt, 1 cucumber (grated), 1 tablespoon dill, salt to taste

Instructions:

1. **Prepare Kebab Mixture**: In a bowl, combine ground beef, grated onion, garlic, spices, salt, and pepper. Mix well.
2. **Form Kebabs**: Divide mixture and shape onto skewers.
3. **Cook Kebabs**: Grill or broil for 10-12 minutes until cooked through.
4. **Make Yogurt Sauce**: In a bowl, mix yogurt, grated cucumber, dill, and salt. Serve alongside kebabs.

Enjoy these flavorful beef dishes! If you need more recipes or details, feel free to ask!

Beef Pot Roast with Vegetables

Ingredients:

- 3-4 lbs beef chuck roast
- Salt and pepper, to taste
- 2 tablespoons olive oil
- 1 onion, chopped
- 3 carrots, chopped
- 3 potatoes, chopped
- 4 cups beef broth
- 2 tablespoons Worcestershire sauce
- 2 cloves garlic, minced
- 1 teaspoon dried thyme
- 2 bay leaves

Instructions:

1. **Preheat Oven**: Preheat the oven to 325°F (165°C).
2. **Season and Brown the Roast**: Season the beef chuck roast with salt and pepper. In a large Dutch oven, heat olive oil over medium-high heat and brown the roast on all sides.
3. **Add Vegetables**: Remove the roast and set aside. In the same pot, add onions, carrots, and potatoes. Sauté for about 5 minutes.
4. **Combine Ingredients**: Return the roast to the pot. Add beef broth, Worcestershire sauce, garlic, thyme, and bay leaves. Bring to a simmer.
5. **Roast**: Cover and place in the oven. Roast for 3-4 hours until the beef is tender. Remove bay leaves before serving.

Smoked Beef Tenderloin

Ingredients:

- 2 lbs beef tenderloin
- Salt and pepper, to taste
- 2 tablespoons olive oil
- 2 teaspoons garlic powder
- 2 teaspoons onion powder
- 1 teaspoon smoked paprika
- Wood chips for smoking (hickory or mesquite)

Instructions:

1. **Prepare Tenderloin**: Trim any excess fat from the beef tenderloin and season with salt, pepper, garlic powder, onion powder, and smoked paprika.
2. **Preheat Smoker**: Preheat your smoker to 225°F (107°C). Add soaked wood chips according to the manufacturer's instructions.
3. **Smoke**: Place the tenderloin in the smoker and smoke for 1.5 to 2 hours, or until the internal temperature reaches 130°F (54°C) for medium-rare.
4. **Rest and Serve**: Remove from smoker, let rest for 10 minutes, then slice and serve.

Beef Tamales

Ingredients:

- 2 lbs beef chuck roast
- 1 onion, chopped
- 4 cloves garlic, minced
- 2 teaspoons chili powder
- 1 teaspoon cumin
- Salt and pepper, to taste
- 2 cups masa harina
- 1/2 cup lard or vegetable shortening
- 1 cup beef broth
- Corn husks (soaked)

Instructions:

1. **Cook the Beef**: In a large pot, cook beef, onion, garlic, chili powder, cumin, salt, and pepper in enough water to cover until tender (about 2-3 hours). Shred the beef and set aside.
2. **Prepare Masa**: In a bowl, beat lard until fluffy. Gradually add masa harina and beef broth, mixing until smooth.
3. **Assemble Tamales**: Take a soaked corn husk, spread masa mixture in the center, top with shredded beef, then fold and tie.
4. **Steam**: Place tamales upright in a steamer and steam for about 1.5 hours, or until masa is firm.

Beef Picadillo

Ingredients:

- 1 lb ground beef
- 1 onion, chopped
- 2 cloves garlic, minced
- 1 bell pepper, chopped
- 1 can (15 oz) diced tomatoes
- 1/2 cup olives, chopped
- 1/4 cup raisins
- 2 teaspoons cumin
- Salt and pepper, to taste

Instructions:

1. **Cook Beef**: In a large skillet, cook ground beef with onion, garlic, and bell pepper over medium heat until beef is browned. Drain excess fat.
2. **Add Ingredients**: Stir in diced tomatoes, olives, raisins, cumin, salt, and pepper.
3. **Simmer**: Cook for 15-20 minutes, allowing flavors to meld. Serve with rice or tortillas.

Beef and Barley Soup

Ingredients:

- 1 lb beef stew meat, cut into cubes
- 1 onion, chopped
- 2 carrots, sliced
- 2 celery stalks, chopped
- 2 cloves garlic, minced
- 6 cups beef broth
- 1 cup pearl barley
- 1 teaspoon thyme
- Salt and pepper, to taste

Instructions:

1. **Brown Beef**: In a large pot, brown the beef stew meat over medium-high heat. Remove and set aside.
2. **Sauté Vegetables**: Add onion, carrots, celery, and garlic to the pot. Sauté until softened.
3. **Combine Ingredients**: Return beef to the pot, add broth, barley, thyme, salt, and pepper. Bring to a boil.
4. **Simmer**: Reduce heat and simmer for 1.5 to 2 hours, or until beef is tender and barley is cooked.

Szechuan Beef with Peppers

Ingredients:

- 1 lb flank steak, thinly sliced
- 2 bell peppers, sliced
- 1 onion, sliced
- 2 tablespoons Szechuan sauce
- 2 tablespoons soy sauce
- 2 cloves garlic, minced
- 1 tablespoon ginger, minced
- 2 tablespoons vegetable oil

Instructions:

1. **Marinate Beef**: In a bowl, combine beef, Szechuan sauce, soy sauce, garlic, and ginger. Let marinate for 15 minutes.
2. **Cook Beef**: In a skillet or wok, heat oil over high heat. Add marinated beef and stir-fry until browned. Remove and set aside.
3. **Stir-Fry Vegetables**: In the same skillet, add bell peppers and onion. Stir-fry for 3-4 minutes until tender.
4. **Combine**: Return beef to the skillet, stir to combine, and cook for an additional 2 minutes.

Beef Casserole with Cheese Topping

Ingredients:

- 1 lb ground beef
- 1 onion, chopped
- 2 cups cooked pasta (elbow or penne)
- 1 can (15 oz) tomato sauce
- 1 teaspoon Italian seasoning
- Salt and pepper, to taste
- 1 cup shredded cheese (cheddar or mozzarella)

Instructions:

1. **Preheat Oven**: Preheat the oven to 350°F (175°C).
2. **Cook Beef**: In a skillet, brown ground beef with onion until fully cooked. Drain excess fat.
3. **Combine Ingredients**: In a large bowl, mix cooked pasta, tomato sauce, Italian seasoning, salt, pepper, and beef mixture.
4. **Assemble Casserole**: Transfer to a baking dish, top with shredded cheese, and bake for 20-25 minutes until cheese is melted and bubbly.

Beef Satay with Peanut Sauce

Ingredients:

- 1 lb beef sirloin, thinly sliced
- 2 tablespoons soy sauce
- 2 tablespoons brown sugar
- 2 teaspoons curry powder
- Skewers (soaked if wooden)
- **For Peanut Sauce**: 1/2 cup peanut butter, 1/4 cup coconut milk, 2 tablespoons soy sauce, 1 tablespoon lime juice, chili flakes to taste

Instructions:

1. **Marinate Beef**: In a bowl, mix soy sauce, brown sugar, and curry powder. Add beef slices and marinate for at least 30 minutes.
2. **Prepare Peanut Sauce**: In a small bowl, whisk together peanut butter, coconut milk, soy sauce, lime juice, and chili flakes. Adjust consistency with water if needed.
3. **Skewer and Grill**: Thread beef onto skewers. Grill over medium heat for about 2-3 minutes per side.
4. **Serve**: Serve skewers with peanut sauce for dipping.

Enjoy preparing these delicious beef recipes! If you have any other requests or need further details, just let me know!

Beef Tartar with Capers

Ingredients:

- 8 oz beef tenderloin, finely chopped
- 2 tablespoons capers, drained and chopped
- 1 tablespoon Dijon mustard
- 1 tablespoon Worcestershire sauce
- 1 small shallot, finely chopped
- Salt and pepper, to taste
- 1 egg yolk (optional)
- Fresh parsley, for garnish
- Crostini or crackers, for serving

Instructions:

1. **Prepare the Beef**: In a mixing bowl, combine chopped beef, capers, Dijon mustard, Worcestershire sauce, shallot, salt, and pepper. Mix until well combined.
2. **Plate the Tartare**: Use a ring mold or shape the mixture into a patty on a plate.
3. **Garnish**: If using, make a small well in the center and add the egg yolk. Garnish with fresh parsley.
4. **Serve**: Serve immediately with crostini or crackers.

Beef and Mushroom Stroganoff

Ingredients:

- 1 lb beef sirloin, sliced thinly
- 8 oz mushrooms, sliced
- 1 onion, chopped
- 2 cloves garlic, minced
- 1 cup beef broth
- 1 cup sour cream
- 2 tablespoons flour
- 2 tablespoons olive oil
- Salt and pepper, to taste
- Egg noodles or rice, for serving

Instructions:

1. **Cook Beef**: In a skillet, heat olive oil over medium-high heat. Sauté the beef until browned. Remove and set aside.
2. **Sauté Vegetables**: In the same skillet, add onions and garlic, cooking until softened. Add mushrooms and cook until they release their moisture.
3. **Make Sauce**: Sprinkle flour over the vegetables and stir. Gradually add beef broth, stirring until thickened.
4. **Combine**: Reduce heat and stir in sour cream. Add the cooked beef back into the skillet and heat through. Season with salt and pepper.
5. **Serve**: Serve over cooked egg noodles or rice.

Beef and Pepper Stir-Fry

Ingredients:

- 1 lb flank steak, sliced thinly against the grain
- 2 bell peppers (any color), sliced
- 1 onion, sliced
- 3 cloves garlic, minced
- 2 tablespoons soy sauce
- 1 tablespoon oyster sauce
- 1 tablespoon vegetable oil
- Salt and pepper, to taste

Instructions:

1. **Marinate Beef**: In a bowl, combine sliced beef, soy sauce, and oyster sauce. Let it marinate for 15 minutes.
2. **Stir-Fry**: In a large skillet or wok, heat vegetable oil over high heat. Add the marinated beef and stir-fry until browned. Remove and set aside.
3. **Cook Vegetables**: In the same skillet, add onions and garlic, cooking until fragrant. Add bell peppers and stir-fry until tender-crisp.
4. **Combine**: Return the beef to the skillet and stir to combine. Season with salt and pepper.
5. **Serve**: Serve hot over rice or noodles.

Thai Red Curry Beef

Ingredients:

- 1 lb beef (flank steak or sirloin), thinly sliced
- 2 tablespoons red curry paste
- 1 can (13.5 oz) coconut milk
- 1 bell pepper, sliced
- 1 cup broccoli florets
- 2 tablespoons fish sauce
- 1 tablespoon brown sugar
- Fresh basil, for garnish
- Jasmine rice, for serving

Instructions:

1. **Cook Beef**: In a skillet, cook sliced beef over medium-high heat until browned.
2. **Add Curry Paste**: Stir in red curry paste and cook for 1 minute until fragrant.
3. **Add Coconut Milk**: Pour in coconut milk, fish sauce, and brown sugar. Stir to combine.
4. **Add Vegetables**: Add bell pepper and broccoli, simmering until vegetables are tender.
5. **Serve**: Serve hot over jasmine rice, garnished with fresh basil.

Beef Empanadas

Ingredients:

- 1 lb ground beef
- 1 onion, chopped
- 2 cloves garlic, minced
- 1 teaspoon cumin
- 1 teaspoon paprika
- Salt and pepper, to taste
- 1 package empanada dough (store-bought)
- 1 egg (for egg wash)

Instructions:

1. **Cook Filling**: In a skillet, cook ground beef with onions and garlic until browned. Stir in cumin, paprika, salt, and pepper. Remove from heat.
2. **Assemble Empanadas**: On a floured surface, roll out empanada dough. Place a spoonful of beef filling on one half, fold over, and crimp edges to seal.
3. **Prepare for Baking**: Preheat the oven to 375°F (190°C). Place empanadas on a baking sheet and brush with beaten egg.
4. **Bake**: Bake for 20-25 minutes, or until golden brown. Serve warm.

Beef Shakshuka

Ingredients:

- 1 lb ground beef
- 1 onion, chopped
- 2 bell peppers, chopped
- 2 cloves garlic, minced
- 1 can (15 oz) crushed tomatoes
- 4 eggs
- 1 teaspoon cumin
- 1 teaspoon paprika
- Salt and pepper, to taste
- Fresh parsley, for garnish

Instructions:

1. **Cook Beef**: In a skillet, cook ground beef with onions, garlic, and bell peppers until the beef is browned.
2. **Add Tomatoes and Spices**: Stir in crushed tomatoes, cumin, paprika, salt, and pepper. Simmer for 10 minutes.
3. **Add Eggs**: Make small wells in the mixture and crack an egg into each well. Cover and cook until eggs are set.
4. **Serve**: Garnish with fresh parsley and serve with crusty bread.

Beef Jalfrezi

Ingredients:

- 1 lb beef sirloin, sliced
- 2 bell peppers, sliced
- 1 onion, sliced
- 3 cloves garlic, minced
- 1 inch ginger, grated
- 2 tablespoons jalfrezi paste
- 1 can (14 oz) diced tomatoes
- 1 tablespoon vegetable oil
- Salt and pepper, to taste

Instructions:

1. **Cook Beef**: Heat oil in a pan and sauté beef until browned. Remove and set aside.
2. **Sauté Vegetables**: In the same pan, add onions, garlic, and ginger. Cook until softened, then add bell peppers and sauté for a few more minutes.
3. **Add Paste and Tomatoes**: Stir in jalfrezi paste and diced tomatoes. Cook for a few minutes.
4. **Combine**: Return the beef to the pan, mixing everything together. Season with salt and pepper.
5. **Serve**: Serve with rice or naan.

Beef Brisket Tacos

Ingredients:

- 2 lbs beef brisket
- 1 onion, sliced
- 2 cloves garlic, minced
- 1 tablespoon chili powder
- 1 teaspoon cumin
- 1 cup beef broth
- Corn tortillas
- Toppings: chopped cilantro, diced onions, lime wedges

Instructions:

1. **Cook Brisket**: In a slow cooker, place brisket, onions, garlic, chili powder, cumin, and beef broth. Cook on low for 8-10 hours until tender.
2. **Shred Beef**: Once cooked, shred the brisket using two forks.
3. **Assemble Tacos**: Warm corn tortillas and fill with shredded brisket.
4. **Serve**: Top with cilantro, onions, and a squeeze of lime.

Beef and Lentil Stew

Ingredients:

- 1 lb beef stew meat, cubed
- 1 cup lentils (green or brown)
- 1 onion, chopped
- 2 carrots, diced
- 2 celery stalks, diced
- 4 cups beef broth
- 2 cloves garlic, minced
- 1 teaspoon thyme
- Salt and pepper, to taste

Instructions:

1. **Brown Beef**: In a large pot, brown beef stew meat over medium-high heat. Remove and set aside.
2. **Sauté Vegetables**: Add onion, carrots, and celery to the pot, cooking until softened. Stir in garlic.
3. **Combine Ingredients**: Add lentils, beef broth, thyme, salt, pepper, and the browned beef.
4. **Simmer**: Bring to a boil, then reduce heat and simmer for about 45 minutes, or until lentils and beef are tender.

Enjoy preparing these flavorful beef dishes! If you need further assistance or additional recipes, just let me know!

Beef and Bacon Burgers

Ingredients:

- 1 lb ground beef
- 4 slices bacon, cooked and chopped
- 1/4 cup breadcrumbs
- 1 egg
- 1 tablespoon Worcestershire sauce
- Salt and pepper, to taste
- Burger buns, for serving
- Toppings: lettuce, tomato, cheese, etc.

Instructions:

1. **Mix Ingredients**: In a large bowl, combine ground beef, chopped bacon, breadcrumbs, egg, Worcestershire sauce, salt, and pepper.
2. **Form Patties**: Shape the mixture into burger patties.
3. **Cook Patties**: Grill or pan-fry the patties over medium heat for about 5-7 minutes per side or until cooked to your desired doneness.
4. **Serve**: Place patties on burger buns and add desired toppings.

Beef and Sweet Potato Hash

Ingredients:

- 1 lb ground beef
- 2 medium sweet potatoes, peeled and diced
- 1 onion, chopped
- 1 bell pepper, chopped
- 2 cloves garlic, minced
- 1 teaspoon paprika
- Salt and pepper, to taste
- Fresh parsley, for garnish

Instructions:

1. **Cook Beef**: In a large skillet, brown the ground beef over medium heat. Remove and set aside.
2. **Sauté Vegetables**: In the same skillet, add sweet potatoes, onions, and bell peppers. Cook until sweet potatoes are tender.
3. **Add Garlic and Spices**: Stir in garlic, paprika, salt, and pepper. Cook for another minute.
4. **Combine**: Return the beef to the skillet, mixing everything together.
5. **Serve**: Garnish with fresh parsley before serving.

Moroccan Beef Tagine

Ingredients:

- 1 lb beef stew meat, cubed
- 1 onion, chopped
- 3 cloves garlic, minced
- 2 cups beef broth
- 1 can (14 oz) diced tomatoes
- 1 cup chickpeas, drained and rinsed
- 2 teaspoons cumin
- 2 teaspoons coriander
- 1 teaspoon cinnamon
- Salt and pepper, to taste
- Fresh cilantro, for garnish

Instructions:

1. **Brown Beef**: In a tagine or large pot, brown beef over medium heat. Remove and set aside.
2. **Sauté Onions**: Add onions and garlic to the pot, cooking until softened.
3. **Add Ingredients**: Stir in beef broth, diced tomatoes, chickpeas, cumin, coriander, cinnamon, salt, and pepper.
4. **Simmer**: Return the beef to the pot and simmer for 1.5 to 2 hours, until beef is tender.
5. **Serve**: Garnish with fresh cilantro before serving.

Beef and Spinach Stuffed Shells

Ingredients:

- 12 jumbo pasta shells
- 1 lb ground beef
- 2 cups fresh spinach, chopped
- 1 cup ricotta cheese
- 1 cup marinara sauce
- 1 cup mozzarella cheese, shredded
- 1/4 cup grated Parmesan cheese
- Salt and pepper, to taste

Instructions:

1. **Preheat Oven**: Preheat the oven to 375°F (190°C).
2. **Cook Pasta**: Cook jumbo shells according to package instructions; drain and set aside.
3. **Cook Beef**: In a skillet, brown ground beef, then add chopped spinach, cooking until wilted. Remove from heat.
4. **Mix Filling**: In a bowl, combine beef mixture, ricotta cheese, salt, and pepper.
5. **Stuff Shells**: Fill each shell with the beef mixture and place in a baking dish. Pour marinara sauce over the shells, then top with mozzarella and Parmesan cheese.
6. **Bake**: Cover with foil and bake for 20 minutes, then remove foil and bake for an additional 10 minutes until cheese is bubbly.

Beef and Avocado Salad

Ingredients:

- 1 lb grilled steak, sliced
- 2 cups mixed salad greens
- 1 avocado, diced
- 1/2 red onion, thinly sliced
- 1 cup cherry tomatoes, halved
- 1/4 cup feta cheese, crumbled
- Olive oil, for dressing
- Salt and pepper, to taste

Instructions:

1. **Prepare Salad**: In a large bowl, combine salad greens, avocado, red onion, cherry tomatoes, and feta cheese.
2. **Add Steak**: Top the salad with sliced grilled steak.
3. **Dress and Serve**: Drizzle with olive oil, season with salt and pepper, and toss gently before serving.

Beef and Artichoke Pasta

Ingredients:

- 8 oz pasta (penne or fusilli)
- 1 lb ground beef
- 1 can (14 oz) artichoke hearts, drained and chopped
- 2 cups spinach
- 2 cloves garlic, minced
- 1/2 cup cream
- 1/2 cup grated Parmesan cheese
- Salt and pepper, to taste

Instructions:

1. **Cook Pasta**: Cook pasta according to package instructions; drain and set aside.
2. **Brown Beef**: In a skillet, brown ground beef over medium heat.
3. **Add Vegetables**: Stir in garlic, artichoke hearts, and spinach, cooking until spinach is wilted.
4. **Mix Sauce**: Pour in cream and stir in Parmesan cheese. Season with salt and pepper.
5. **Combine**: Add the cooked pasta to the skillet, mixing everything together. Serve hot.

Beef Rendang

Ingredients:

- 2 lbs beef chuck, cut into cubes
- 1 can (13.5 oz) coconut milk
- 1 onion, chopped
- 3 cloves garlic, minced
- 1 inch ginger, grated
- 2 tablespoons rendang curry paste
- 2 tablespoons brown sugar
- 1 tablespoon tamarind paste
- Salt, to taste

Instructions:

1. **Brown Beef**: In a large pot, brown the beef over medium heat.
2. **Add Aromatics**: Add onion, garlic, ginger, and rendang curry paste, stirring until fragrant.
3. **Simmer**: Pour in coconut milk, brown sugar, tamarind paste, and salt. Bring to a boil, then reduce heat and simmer for 2-3 hours, until beef is tender.
4. **Serve**: Serve with steamed rice.

Enjoy preparing these delicious beef recipes! If you need more assistance or additional recipes, just let me know!